2ND GRADE
MATH
INTERACTIVE NOTEBOOK

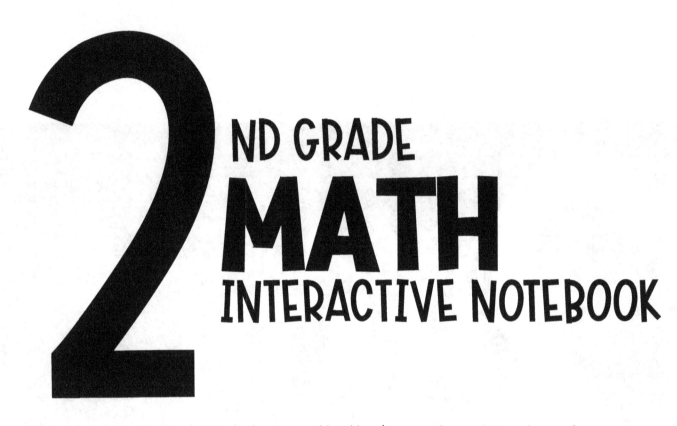

2ND GRADE MATH INTERACTIVE NOTEBOOK

Our goal is to help you Work Smarter, Not Harder, so please let us know how we can help you by emailing at contact@SmithCurriculumConsulting.com

If you are a teacher, or school, using these practice sheets for students, you must purchase a school license to get permission for classroom use. Please email us at contact@SmithCurriculumConsulting.com to obtain a school license.

TEACHER INFO:

Thank you for your purchase of the Second Math Interactive Notebook Unit. Within this workbook are a total of 51 complete lessons for you to use in your math lessons and interactive notebooks.

The book is set up with printables for each lesson. Each of the printables are single-sided in the workbook to provide for the ability to be used in a homeschool setting as well or torn out by a teacher and easily copied.

All the included lessons have been aligned to Texas Essential Knowledge and Skills (TEKS) and Common Core State Standards (CCSS). Due to this alignment, you may find that some lessons do not apply to your grade level, but they have been left in the unit to cover standards that they match for others.

We would love to see how you are using this in your setting so please feel free to tag us on Instagram (@JenniferSJochen) or Facebook (@Smith Curriculum and Consulting) so we can see your work!

TEACHER INFO:

Page	Lesson Title	TEKS	CCSS
9	Showing Place Value (to tens)	2.2a	2.NBT1
11	Showing Place Value (to hundreds)	2.2a	2.NBT1
13	Bundling Numbers	2.2a	2.NBT1
15	Base Ten Match Up	2.2a	2.NBT1
19	Count by 5s	2.2a	2.NBT.2
21	Count by 10s	2.2a	2.NBT.2
23	Count by 100s	2.2a	2.NBT.2
25	Representing Numbers	2.2b	2.NBT.3
27	Comparing Numbers	2.2d	2.NBT.4
31	Ordering Numbers	2.2d	2.NBT.4
33	How Many Flavors?	2.10b, 2.10d	2.MD10
35	How Do You Get Home?	2.10b, 2.10d	2.MD10
37	Adding Within 100	2.4c	2.OA1
39	Subtracting Within 100	2.4c	2.OA1

TEACHER INFO:

Page	Lesson Title	TEKS	CCSS
41	Fact Families	2.4a	2.OA.2
45	Doubles Plus One	2.4a	2.OA.2
47	Doubles Minus One	2.4a	2.OA.2
49	How Much In A Name?	2.4d	2.NBT.5
51	Missing Number Match Up	2.4d	2.NBT.5
53	Spending Money	2.5a	2.MD.8
55	Favorite Superhero	2.10b, 2.10d	2.MD10
57	Adding Big Numbers	2.4b	2.NBT.6
61	Adding Within 100	2.4b	2.NBT.7
63	Subtracting Within 100	2.4b	2.NBT.7
65	Composing Tens	2.2a	2.NBT.7
67	Decomposing Tens	2.2a	2.NBT.7
69	Skip Count by 10s	2.2a	2.NBT.8
71	Skip Count by 100s	2.2a	2.NBT.8

TEACHER INFO:

Page	Lesson Title	TEKS	CCSS
73	Open Ended CGI	2.7c	2.NBT.9
75	Piggy Bank Totals	2.5a, 2.5b	2.MD.8
77	Estimate & Measure	2.9d	2.MD1, 2.MD.3
79	Playground Estimation	2.9d	2.MD1, 2.MD.3
81	Measuring Twice	2.9d	2.MD.2
83	Length of Lines	2.9d	2.MD.4
85	Measurement Word Problems	2.9e	2.MD.5
87	Solving with Number Lines	2.9c, 2.2e, 2.2f	2.MD.6
89	AM or PM Sort	2.9g	2.MD.7
91	It's About Time	2.9g	2.MD.7
93	Measure & Plot	2.9d, 2.10b	2.MD9
95	Favorite Subject	2.10b, 2.10d	2.MD10
97	Constructing Shapes	2.8a	2.G1
99	Pieces of a Whole	2.3a	2.G.2

TEACHER INFO:

Page	Lesson Title	TEKS	CCSS
101	Let's Eat Cake	2.8e	2.G.3
103	Types of Shoes	2.10b, 2.10d	2.MD10
105	Creating with Shapes	2.8a, 2.8c, 2.8d, 2.8e	2.G1, 2.G.2, 2.G.3
107	Odd & Even Sort	2.7a	2.OA.3
109	Odd & Even Roll	2.7a, 2.10b	2.OA.3, 2.MD10
111	Building Arrays	2.9f	2.OA4
113	Acting Out Multiplication	2.9f	2.OA4
115	Array Match Up	2.9f	2.OA4
117	What's On Your Pizza?	2.10b, 2.10d	2.MD10

Showing Place Value (to Tens)

Directions: Cut out the rectangle below. Fold on the solid line and staple on each edge as well as in the center. Cut out the number cards to use to display numbers in your place value foldable.

Directions: Cut the foldable on the dashed lines. Fold on the solid lines.

This side should be facing your notebook when glues in and will not be seen.

Ones | Tens

0	9	4	5	8
1	2	5	6	7
2	3	9	8	
3	4	7	1	

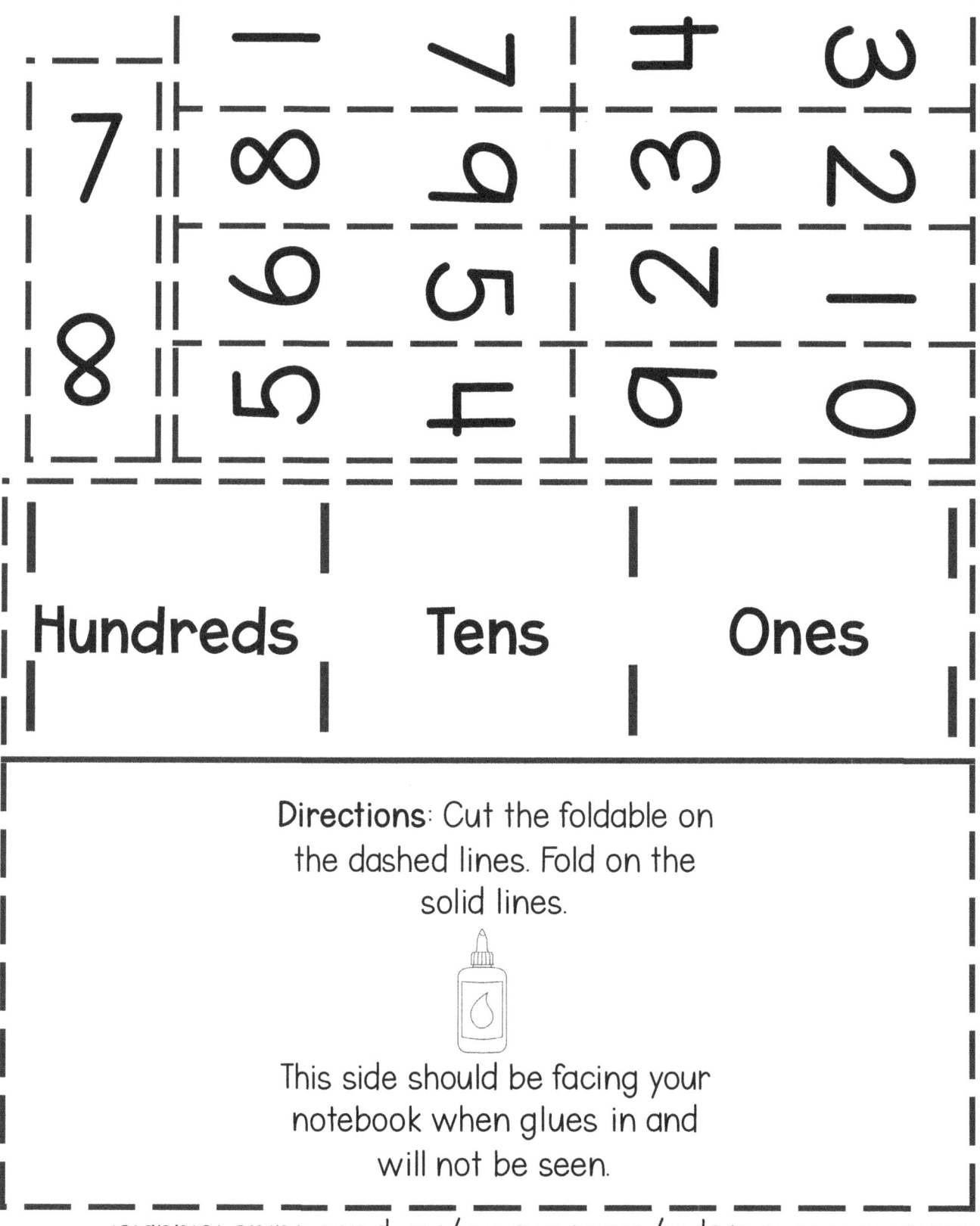

Hundreds   **Tens**   **Ones**

Directions: Cut the foldable on the dashed lines. Fold on the solid lines.

This side should be facing your notebook when glues in and will not be seen.

Showing Place Value (to Hundreds)

Directions: Cut out the rectangle below. Fold on the solid line and staple on each edge as well as in the center. Cut out the number cards to use to display numbers in your place value foldable.

Bundling Numbers

Directions: Cut out each of the mini flap books. Glue under the flap and put it in your notebook. Read the equation on the front and rewrite it in a new way under the flap.

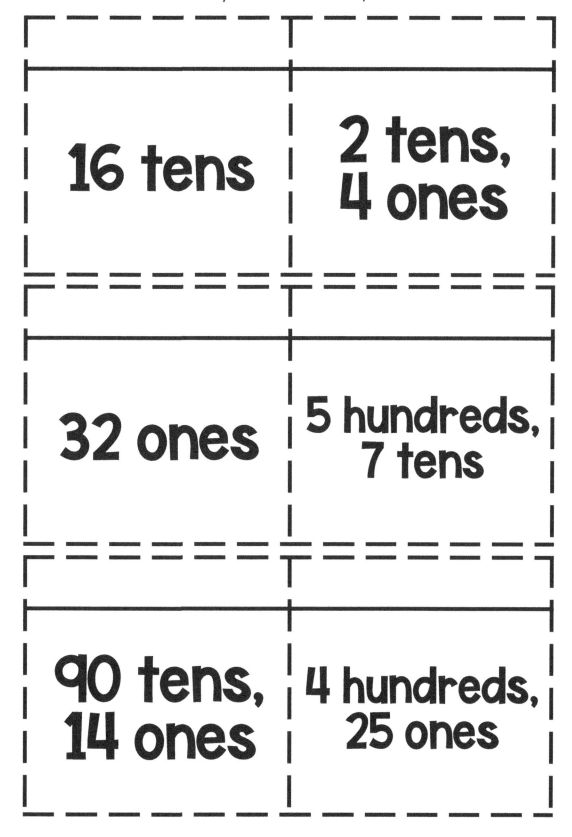

16 tens

2 tens,
4 ones

32 ones

5 hundreds,
7 tens

90 tens,
14 ones

4 hundreds,
25 ones

Base Ten Matchup

Directions: Cut out each of the cards below as well as on page 2. Match the base ten representation with the numeric representation and glue them into your notebook.

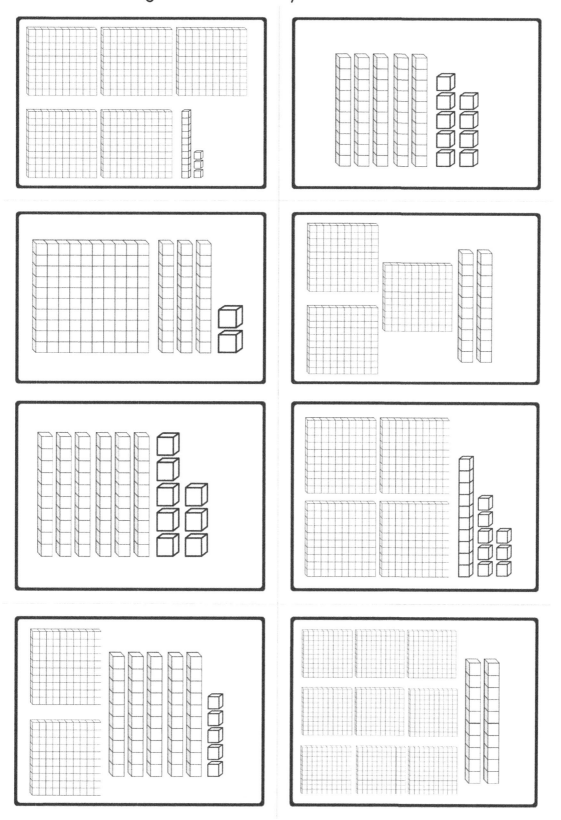

Base Ten Matchup

Directions: Cut out each of the cards below as well as on the previous page. Match the base ten representation with the numeric representation and glue them into your notebook.

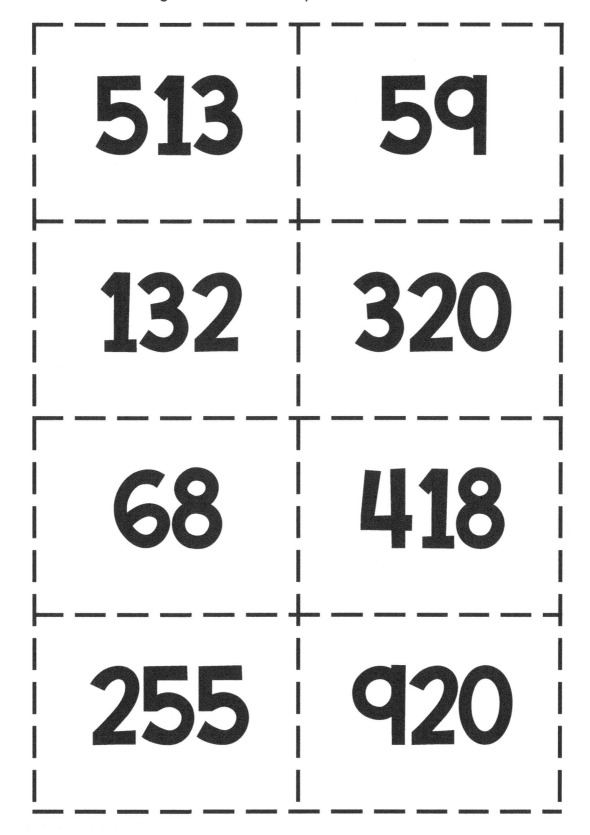

513	59
132	320
68	418
255	920

Count by 5's

Directions: Cut out the grid below and glue it into your notebook. Cut out each of the pieces below and glue them in the correct location by counting by 5's.

5			20
		55	
	70		

15	25	35	45
65	75	10	30
40	50	60	80

Count by 10's

Directions: Cut out the grid below and glue it into your notebook. Cut out each of the pieces below and glue them in the correct location by counting by 10's.

	20		
50		70	
		110	

10	30	40	60
80	90	100	120
130	140	150	160

Count by 100's

Directions: Cut out each of the strips below. Glue them into your notebook. Determine the missing numbers in the sequence by counting by 100's.

100, _____, 300, _____, 500, _____

200, _____, 400, _____, 600, _____

300, _____, _____, 600, _____, _____

_____, _____, 500, _____, 700, _____

400, 500, _____, _____, _____, _____

_____, 300, _____, _____, 600, _____

_____, _____, 700, _____, 900, _____

Representing Numbers

Directions: Cut out each of the grids below. Choose four three-digit numbers and write them in each numeral section. Continue by showing the different representations of each number. Glue into your notebook.

Numeral	Word Form	Base Ten	Expanded Form
Numeral	Word Form	Base Ten	Expanded Form
Numeral	Word Form	Base Ten	Expanded Form
Numeral	Word Form	Base Ten	Expanded Form

Comparing Numbers

Directions: Cut out each of the pockets below. Glue down in your notebook on the tabs. Cut out the number expressions on the next page to complete the task.

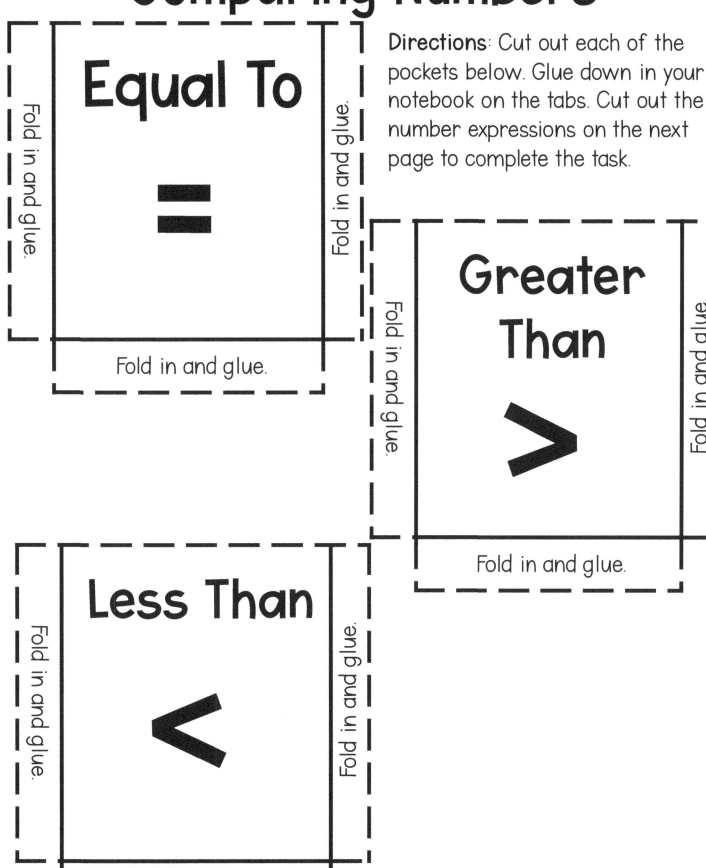

Equal To

=

Fold in and glue.

Fold in and glue.

Fold in and glue.

Greater Than

>

Fold in and glue.

Fold in and glue.

Fold in and glue.

Less Than

<

Fold in and glue.

Fold in and glue.

Fold in and glue.

Comparing Numbers

Directions: Cut out each of the number expressions below. Compare the two numbers or pictures to determine if they are greater than, less than, or equal to. Fill in the space between with the correct symbol and tuck in the pocket that they belong.

214 ___ 238

303 ___ 303

118 ___ 116

651 ___ 656

814 ___ 718

166 ___ 156

471 ___ 470

756 ___ 749

479 ___ 475

286 ___ 232

535 ___ 623

419 ___ 419

Ordering Numbers

Directions: Cut out each of the flap books below. Glue under the flap into your notebook. Read the numbers on the flap and write the numbers in order from least to greatest under the flap.

231, 203, 321	614, 460, 613
789, 798, 897	547, 514, 549
132, 143, 123	396, 316, 406

How Many Flavors?

Directions: Cut out the graph and journal and glue them into your notebook. Survey your classmates to see how their favorite ice cream. Draw a picture for each student who likes that flavor. Answer the journal question based on your data.

What's Your Favorite Flavor?

chocolate   vanilla   strawberry

Our class has _____ who like chocolate, _____ who like vanilla, and _____ who like strawberry. The difference between the largest and smallest is _____.

How Do You Get Home?

Directions: Cut out the graph and journal and glue them into your notebook. Survey your classmates to see how they get home and complete the bar graph. Answer the journal question based on your data.

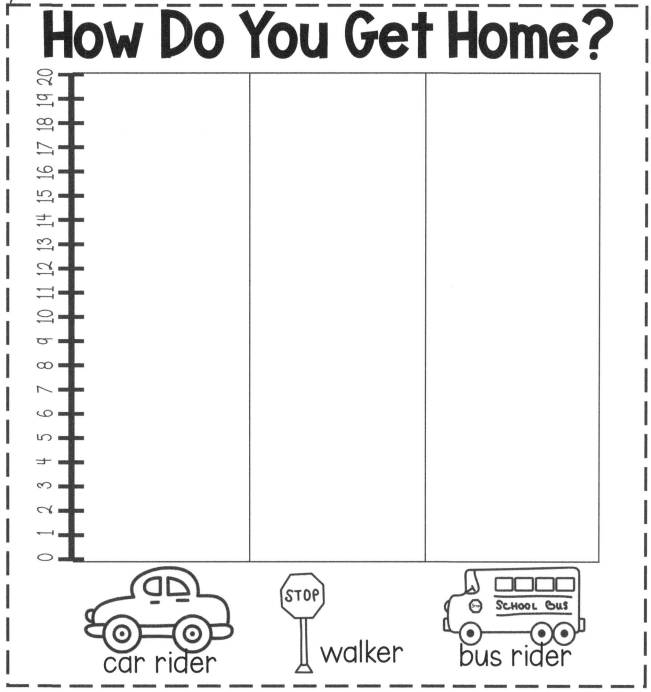

How Do You Get Home?

Our class has _____ car riders, _____ walkers, and _____ bus riders. More students get home by _____.

Adding Within 100

Directions: Cut out the foldable along the dashed lines. Glue the word problem on the back side of the top problem. Illustrate and solve each word problem.

Adding Within 100

Tianna organized all her stuffed animals on her bookshelf. As a reward, her grandmother bought her 4 more animals. Now Tianna has 51 animals. How many animals did Tianna start with?

Samantha wanted to count how many stickers she had earned. She counted 53 owl stickers and 24 star stickers. How many stickers does Samantha have altogether?

Evan had 42 toy cars. For his birthday he received 24 more toy cars. How many toy cars does Evan now have?

Mrs. Knox had 18 students in her class. A teacher got sick, and she gained 8 more students for the day. How many students does Mrs. Know now have in her class?

Subtracting Within 100

Directions: Cut out the foldable along the dashed lines. Glue the word problem on the back side of the top problem. Illustrate and solve each word problem.

Subtracting Within 100

Juan had a total of 83 nickels in his piggy bank. He went to the store and spent some nickels on some candy. Now Juan has 43 nickels left in his piggy bank. How many nickels did Juan spend on candy?

Jordan scored 28 points during his basketball game on Saturday. He scored 31 points in his basketball game on Tuesday. How many more points did Jordan score on Tuesday than on Saturday?

Mrs. Johnson made a total of 144 cookies for the class bake sale. After one hour she had sold 28 cookies. How many cookies were remaining?

At the beginning of the school year, Kylie had a box of pencils. In six weeks, she lost 12 pencils. Kylie now has 44 pencils left. How many pencils did she begin the year with?

Fact Families

Directions: Cut out each of the houses below. Glue them into your notebook. Read the number sentence and write the answer to the first number sentence. Use that to complete the flipped fact.

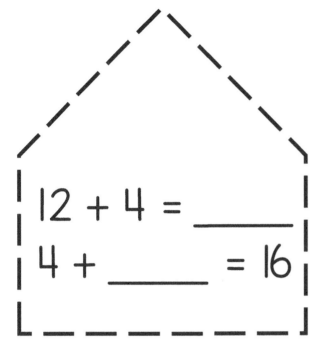

12 + 4 = _____

4 + _____ = 16

6 + 13 = _____

13 + _____ = 19

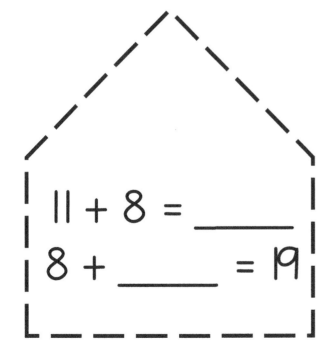

11 + 8 = _____

8 + _____ = 19

5 + 12 = _____

12 + _____ = 17

Fact Families

Directions: Cut out each of the houses below. Glue them into your notebook. Read the number sentence and write the answer to the first number sentence. Use that to complete the flipped fact.

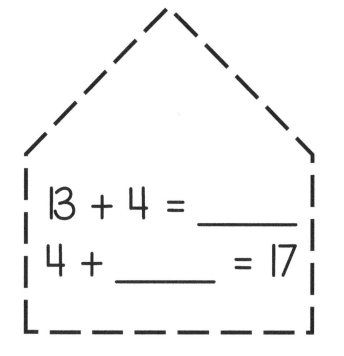

$$13 + 4 = \underline{\hspace{2cm}}$$
$$4 + \underline{\hspace{2cm}} = 17$$

$$9 + 6 = \underline{\hspace{2cm}}$$
$$6 + \underline{\hspace{2cm}} = 15$$

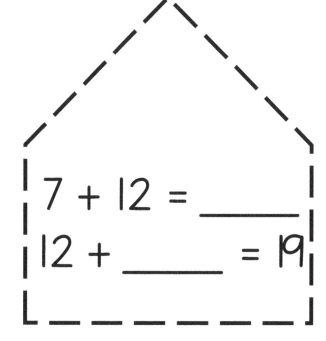

$$7 + 12 = \underline{\hspace{2cm}}$$
$$12 + \underline{\hspace{2cm}} = 19$$

$$9 + 2 = \underline{\hspace{2cm}}$$
$$2 + \underline{\hspace{2cm}} = 11$$

Directions:

Doubles Plus One

Directions: Cut out each of the chocolate pieces below as well as the candy box. Glue the candy box into your notebook and the pieces arranged on top. Solve each of the facts on the candy pieces.

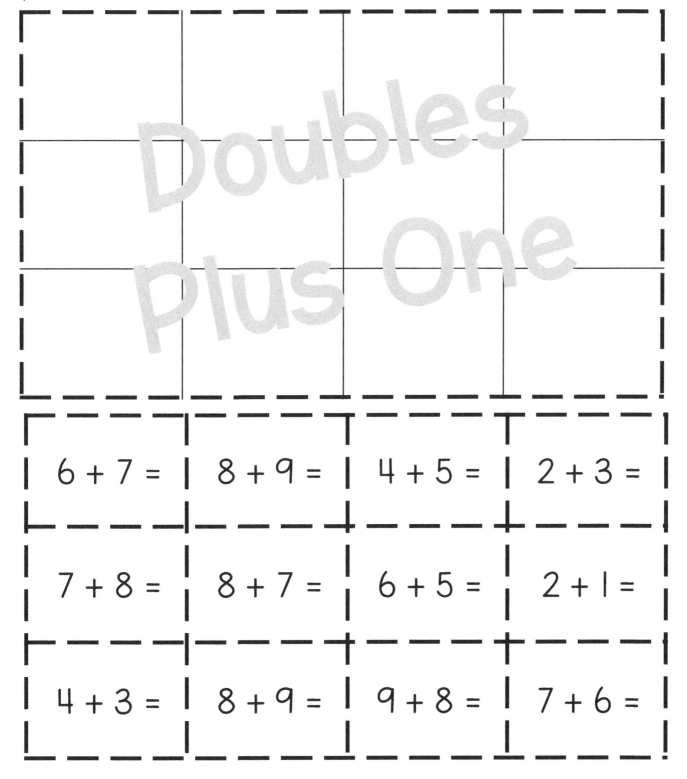

6 + 7 =	8 + 9 =	4 + 5 =	2 + 3 =
7 + 8 =	8 + 7 =	6 + 5 =	2 + 1 =
4 + 3 =	8 + 9 =	9 + 8 =	7 + 6 =

Doubles Minus One

Directions: Cut out each of the chocolate pieces below as well as the candy box. Glue the candy box into your notebook and the pieces arranged on top. Solve each of the facts on the candy pieces.

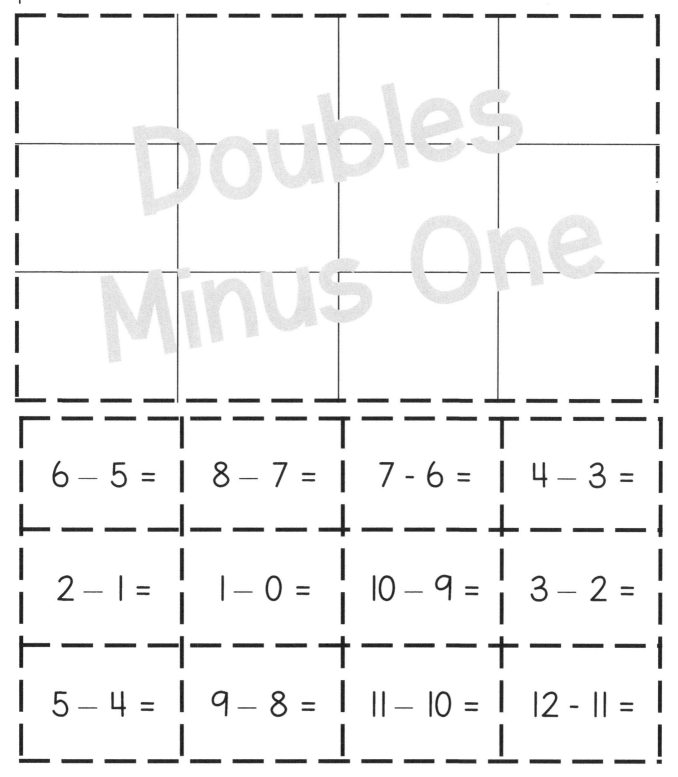

6 − 5 =	8 − 7 =	7 - 6 =	4 − 3 =
2 − 1 =	1 − 0 =	10 − 9 =	3 − 2 =
5 − 4 =	9 − 8 =	11 − 10 =	12 - 11 =

How Much in a Name?

Directions: Cut out the chart and response area below. Glue them into your notebook. Read the questions in the response area and complete them in your notebook.

A	B	C	D	E	F	G	H	I	J	K	L	M
1	2	3	4	5	6	7	8	9	10	11	12	13
N	O	P	Q	R	S	T	U	V	W	X	Y	Z
14	15	16	17	18	19	20	21	22	23	24	25	26

What is your first name?

How much is each letter of your name worth?

What is the total value of your name?

Find someone in your class that has a name that is valued less than your name. Who was it?

Find someone in your class that has a name that is valued more than your name. Who was it?

Was there anyone in your class that had the same value of their names?

49

Missing Number Matchup

Directions: Cut out the foldable below. Glue the tab down into your notebook. Show your work for each number sentence under the flap and write your answer on the top of the flap when complete.

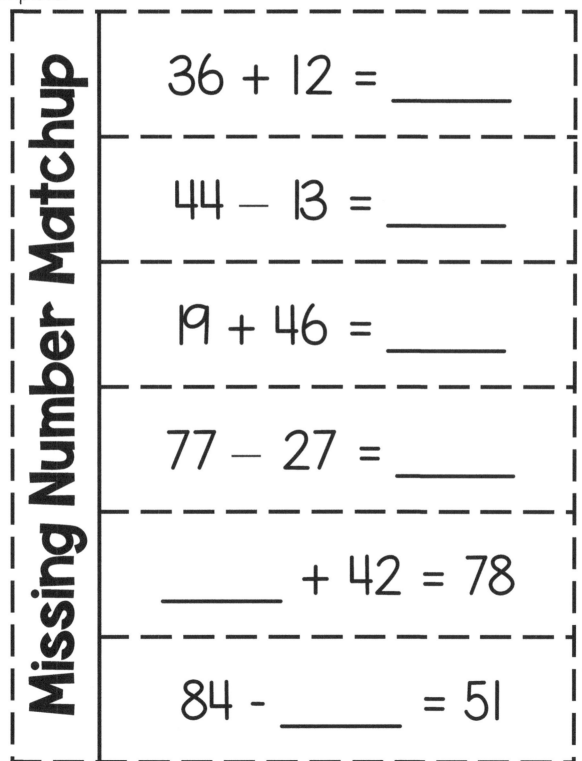

Missing Number Matchup

$36 + 12 =$ _____

$44 - 13 =$ _____

$19 + 46 =$ _____

$77 - 27 =$ _____

_____ $+ 42 = 78$

$84 -$ _____ $= 51$

Spending Money

Directions: Cut out the foldable below on the dashed lines. Glue the title section into your notebook. Read each flap to determine the total of the coins given. Show your work under the flap and circle your answer.

Spending Money

3 quarters, 2 dimes

9 nickels, I dime

I quarter, I dime,
I nickel, I penny

2 nickels, 14 pennies

4 dimes, 2 nickels,
3 pennies

2 quarters, 2 dimes,
2 pennies

3 nickels, 2 dimes, I penny

4 pennies, 3 dimes,
2 nickels, I quarter

Favorite Superhero

Directions: Cut out the bar graph and journal below. Ask the students in your class which of the three superheroes are their favorite and mark it on the bar graph. Answer the journal responses once complete.

Favorite Superhero

| Batman | Captain America | Superman |

Our favorite class superhero is _____ and _____ came in second place. The difference between most and least liked is _____.

Adding Big Numbers

Directions: Cut out each of the mini books below. Glue into your notebook along the flap. Show your work under the flap for each BIG NUMBER addition problem.

```
   44              11
   18              15
 + 10            + 18
```

```
   14              29
   42              31
 + 12            + 14
```

```
   23              12
   15              22
 + 27            + 24
```

Adding Big Numbers

Directions: Cut out each of the mini books below. Glue into your notebook along the flap. Show your work under the flap for each BIG NUMBER addition problem.

```
   16          23
   32          24
+  12       +  25
_____      _____
```

```
   30          51
   19          10
+  25       +  23
_____      _____
```

```
   63          34
   16          25
+  21       +  22
_____      _____
```

Adding Within 100

Directions: Cut out the foldable below. Read the word problem on each flap. Draw a picture and write a number sentence to solve each problem under the flap. Glue into your notebook.

Myra has a quarter, two dimes, and three pennies in her piggy bank. How much money does she have in all?

Mom had already baked 72 cookies for the class bake sale. She made one more batch of 24 cookies to finish it off. How many total cookies did she bake?

Directions: Cut the foldable on the dashed lines. Fold on the solid lines.

This side should be facing your notebook when glues in and will not be seen.

On the first day of school, Thomas was 57 inches tall. When he went to the doctor, they measured him 19 inches taller. How many inches tall is Thomas?

Morgan counted 24 chickens in the pen at the petting zoo. When he went into the barn, he counted another 15 chickens. How many total chickens were there at the petting zoo?

Subtracting Within 100

Directions: Cut out the foldable below. Read the word problem on each flap. Draw a picture and write a number sentence to solve each problem under the flap. Glue into your notebook.

Danny has 52 blue cars and 27 red cars. He gives away 21 cars. How many cars does Danny have left in his collection?

Terry put 56 cups of juice out on the table for her party. When she came back, she noticed that 28 of the cups were gone. How many cups were left on the table?

This side should be facing your notebook when glues in and will not be seen.

Directions: Cut the foldable on the dashed lines. Fold on the solid lines.

Michelle took a typing test and was able to type 34 words per minute. After a month she took another test and was able to type 51 words per minute. What was the change in her words per minute?

Mrs. Anderson counted that she told her students "Use Your Resources" 78 times over one week. The next week she only said it 41 times. How many fewer times did she say it in week two?

Composing Tens

Directions: Cut out the foldable below and glue along the backside into your notebook. Read the number on each flap. Illustrate two ways to create that number using base ten blocks under the flap.

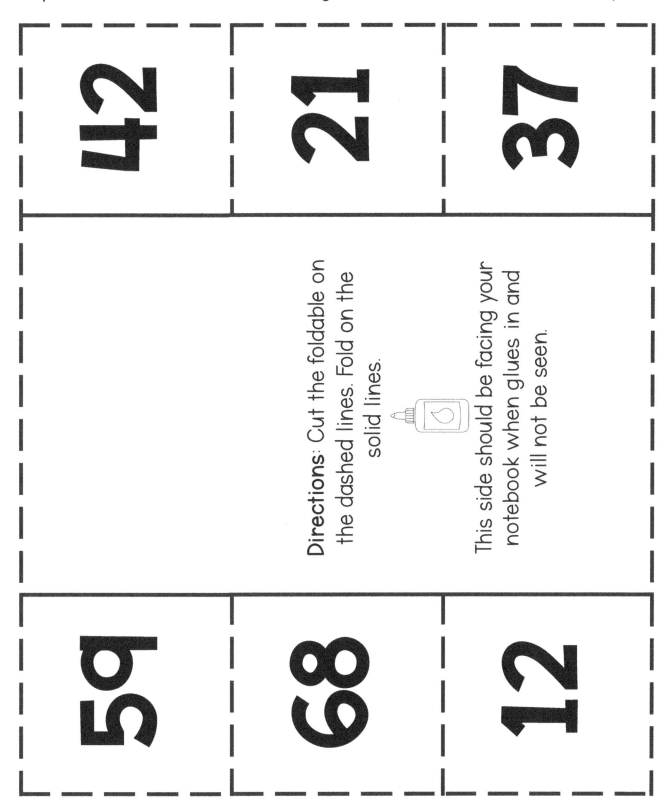

Directions: Cut the foldable on the dashed lines. Fold on the solid lines.

This side should be facing your notebook when glues in and will not be seen.

Decomposing Tens

Directions: Cut out the foldable below and glue it along the backside into your notebook. Read the number on each flap. Create two number sentences using addition under the flap that equals the sum on the front of the flap.

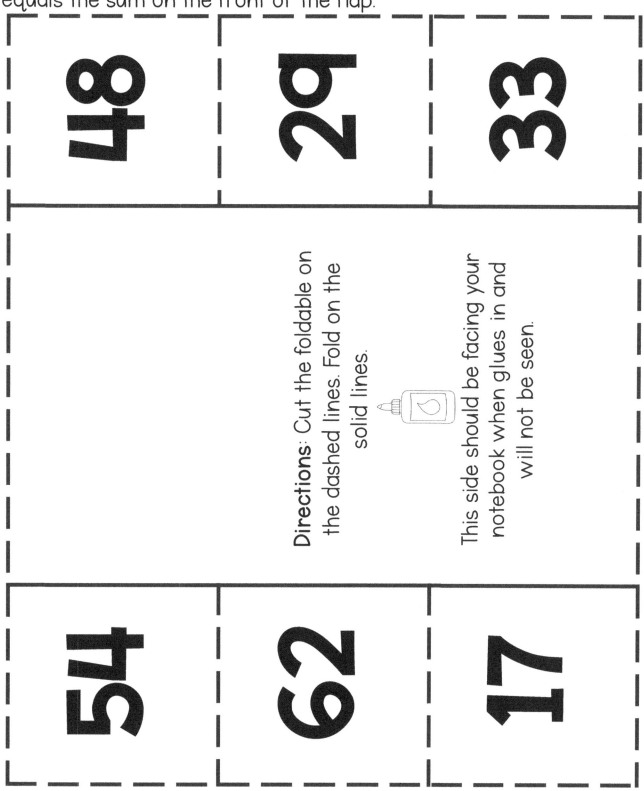

48

29

33

Directions: Cut the foldable on the dashed lines. Fold on the solid lines.

This side should be facing your notebook when glues in and will not be seen.

54

62

17

Skip Count by Tens

Directions: Fill in the missing numbers on the lily pads below. Cut out the number lines on the dotted lines and glue them into your notebook.

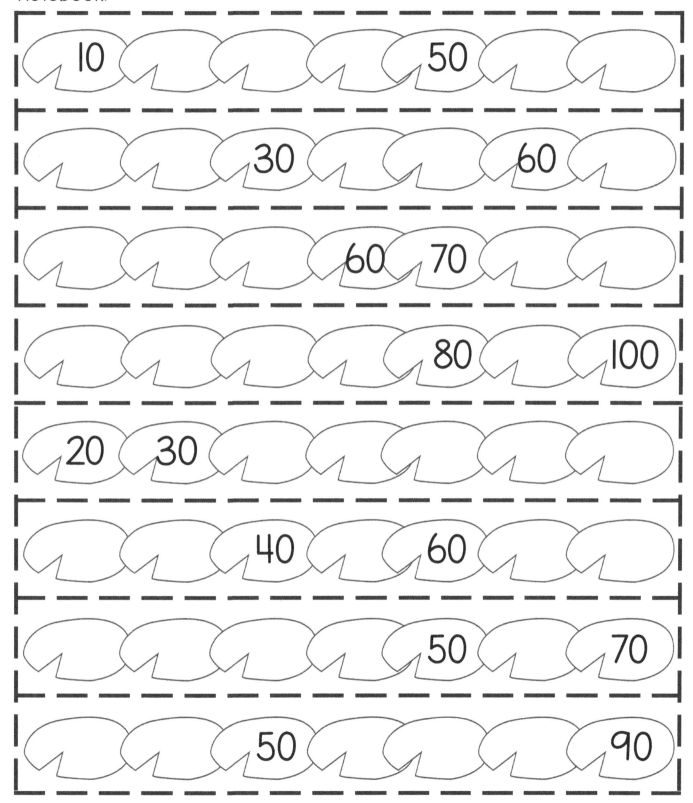

Skip Count by Hundreds

Directions: Fill in the missing numbers on the lily pads below. Cut out the number lines on the dotted lines and glue them into your notebook.

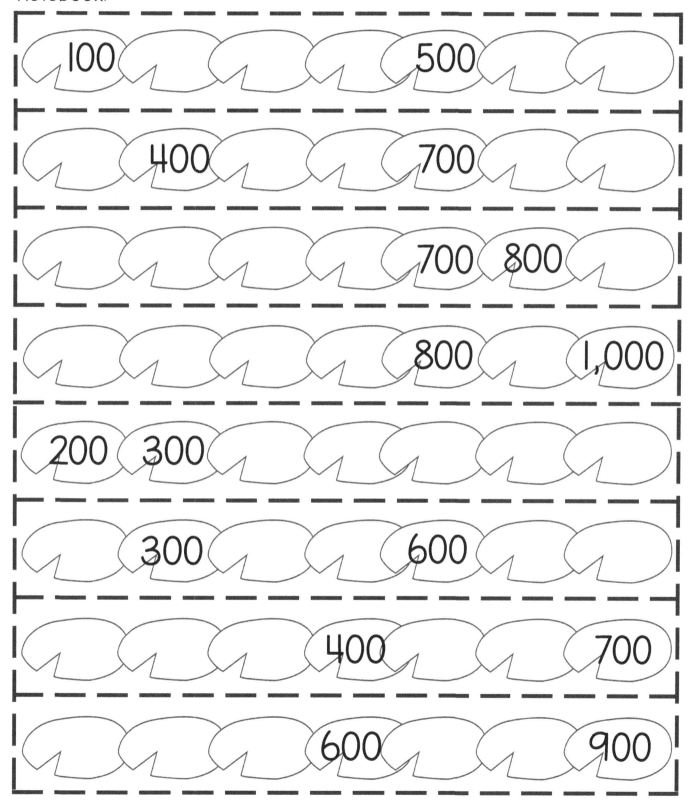

Row 1: 100, ___, ___, ___, 500, ___, ___
Row 2: ___, 400, ___, ___, 700, ___, ___
Row 3: ___, ___, ___, ___, 700, 800, ___
Row 4: ___, ___, ___, ___, 800, ___, 1,000
Row 5: 200, 300, ___, ___, ___, ___, ___
Row 6: ___, 300, ___, ___, 600, ___, ___
Row 7: ___, ___, ___, 400, ___, ___, 700
Row 8: ___, ___, ___, 600, ___, ___, 900

Open Ended CGI

Directions: Cut out the foldable below. Glue into your notebook. Read the problem on the front of the foldable and solve it by showing your work on the inside of your foldable. Write a sentence about your work when you have finished.

Open Ended Word Problems

Macy counted the stickers that she had earned on her sticker chart and came up with 21 stickers. She had some that were hearts and some that were stars. How many of each type of sticker could there be? Show your work.

Piggy Bank Totals

Directions: Cut out the foldable below. Glue the center section down into your notebook. Count the coins in the piggy bank on each flap. Show your work and write the total underneath the flap.

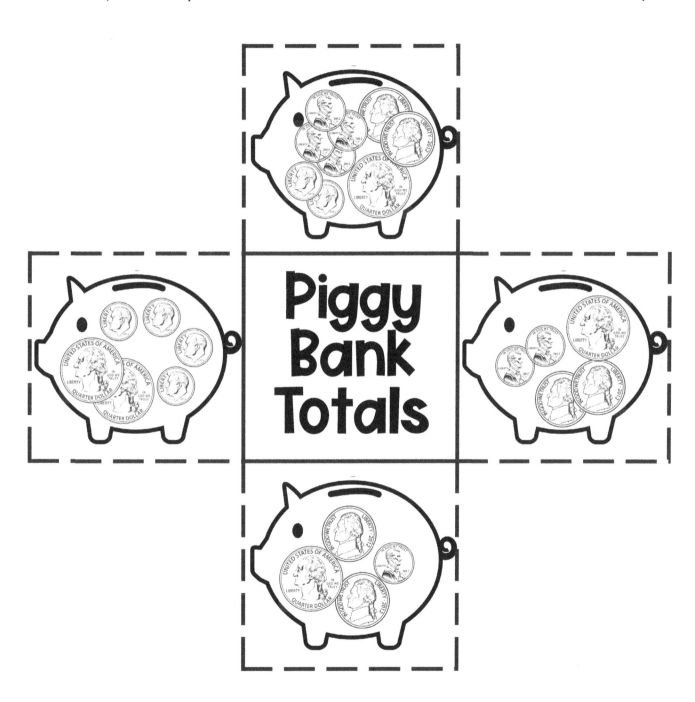

Estimate & Measure

Directions: Cut out the foldable below on the dashed lines and glue it into your notebook. Estimate the measurement of each item on the flap in inches and write that on the inside of your flap. Measure each item with a ruler to the nearest inch and write the correct measurement under the flap. Write a complete sentence about your observations in your notebook.

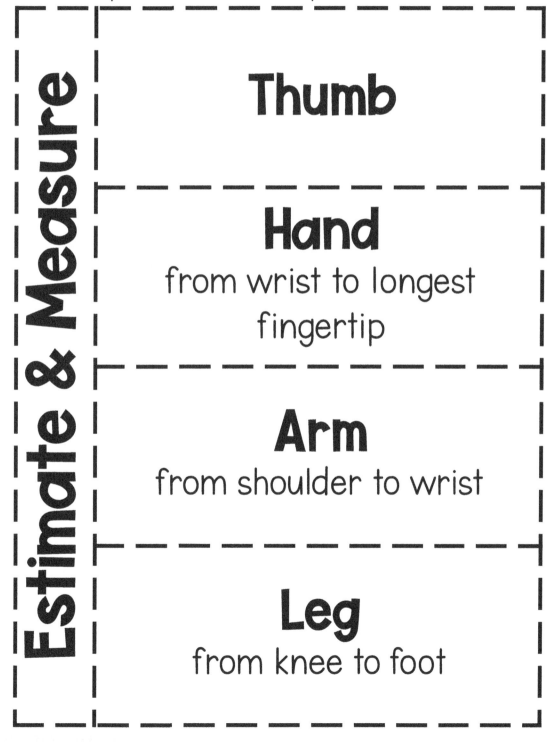

Estimate & Measure

Thumb

Hand
from wrist to longest fingertip

Arm
from shoulder to wrist

Leg
from knee to foot

Playground Estimation

Directions: Take a walk of your playground and sketch where things are located on the graph paper below. Compare your drawing with actual measurements using a meter stick or measuring tape. Create observations about your drawing in your notebook.

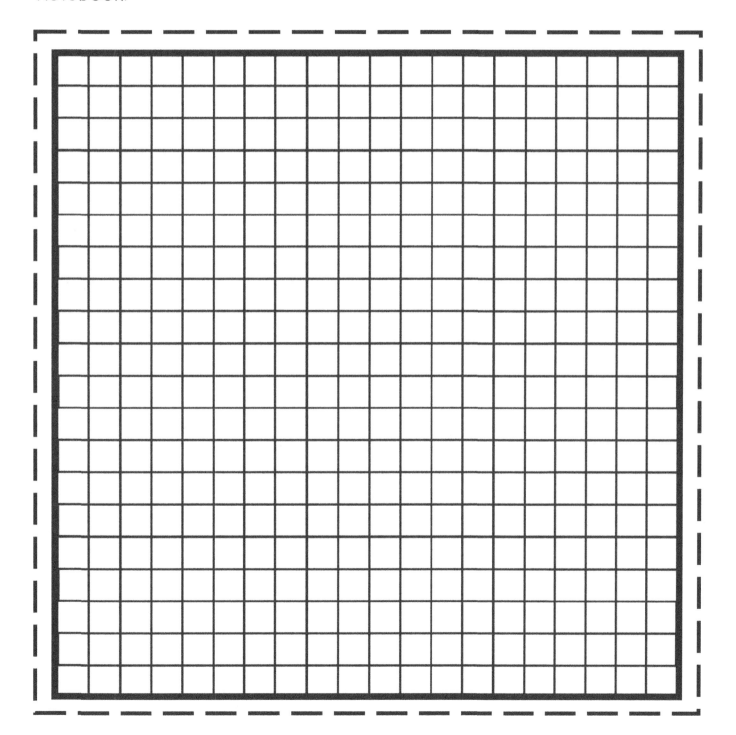

Measuring Twice

Directions: Cut out the staggered book below. Cut out each page and layer on top of each other according to size. Staple where indicated. Directions are given on each page.

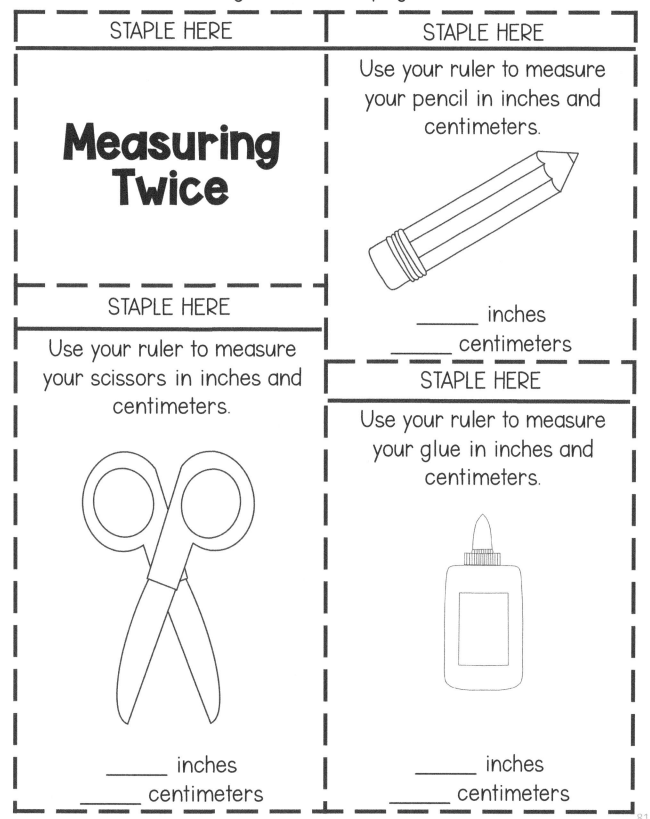

STAPLE HERE

STAPLE HERE

Measuring Twice

Use your ruler to measure your pencil in inches and centimeters.

STAPLE HERE

Use your ruler to measure your scissors in inches and centimeters.

_____ inches

_____ centimeters

STAPLE HERE

Use your ruler to measure your glue in inches and centimeters.

_____ inches

_____ centimeters

_____ inches

_____ centimeters

Length of Lines

Directions: Cut out the foldable below and glue it into your notebook along the side tab. Using your ruler measure each line on the flap to the nearest inch. Under the flap write which line is longer and how much longer it is than the other line.

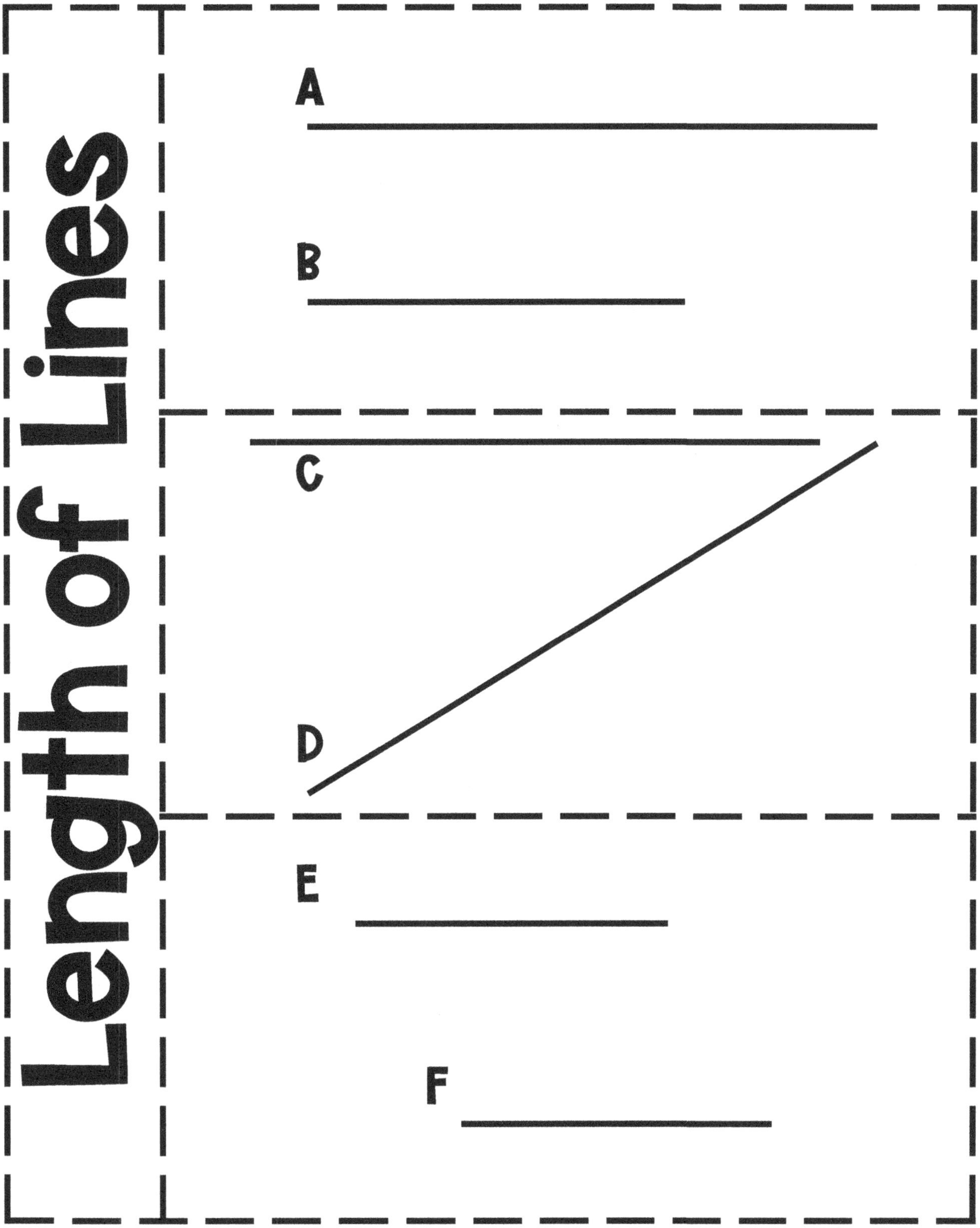

Length of Lines

A _____

B _____

C _____

D

E _____

F _____

Measurement Word Problems

Directions: Cut out the foldable below on the dashed lines and glue it under the title section. Read the word problem on each flap. Use drawings and equations to represent the problem under the flap and solve.

Measurement Word Problems

Sean ran and jumped and was able to jump 34 inches. Jayden did the same and jumped 27 inches. What was the difference in their jumps?

Nick threw the football 18 meters on his first try and 21 meters on his second try. How many meters did he throw the football in all?

Diana needed two pieces of string that were the same length. She measured the first at 39 centimeters and the second at 42 centimeters. How much longer was the second string?

Solving with Number Lines

Directions: Cut out the mini books below. Follow the directions on the back of each mini-book. Glue them into your notebook.

Use the number line to help you solve the subtraction sentence. Show your work on the inside of the mini book.

30 – 13 = _____

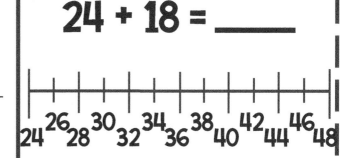

Use the number line to help you solve the addition sentence. Show your work on the inside of the mini-book.

24 + 18 = _____

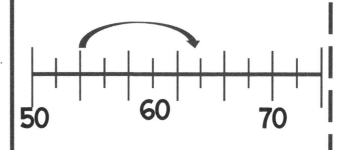

Look at the number line. Fill in the missing numbers on the number line. Write the number sentence that the number line shows and solve inside the mini book.

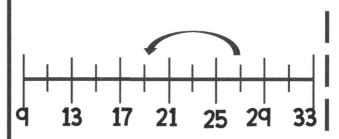

Look at the number line. Fill in the missing numbers on the number line. Write the number sentence that the number line shows and solve inside the mini book.

AM or PM Sort

Directions: On the 12 small cards illustrate an image to match the label. Cut all the cards out as well as the labels. Sort the cards into the given groups based on their common attribute. Use the labels to title your sorts before attaching to the notebook.

Eat Breakfast	Eat Dinner	Take a Bath
Watch Cartoons	Play Outside	Get Out of Bed
Do Chores	Put on Pajamas	Get Dressed
Say the Pledge	Do Homework	Play With Pets

A.M.   P.M.

Its About Time

Directions: Cut out the foldable below. Read the clock and write the time underneath the flap. Describe what you might do at that time of the day.

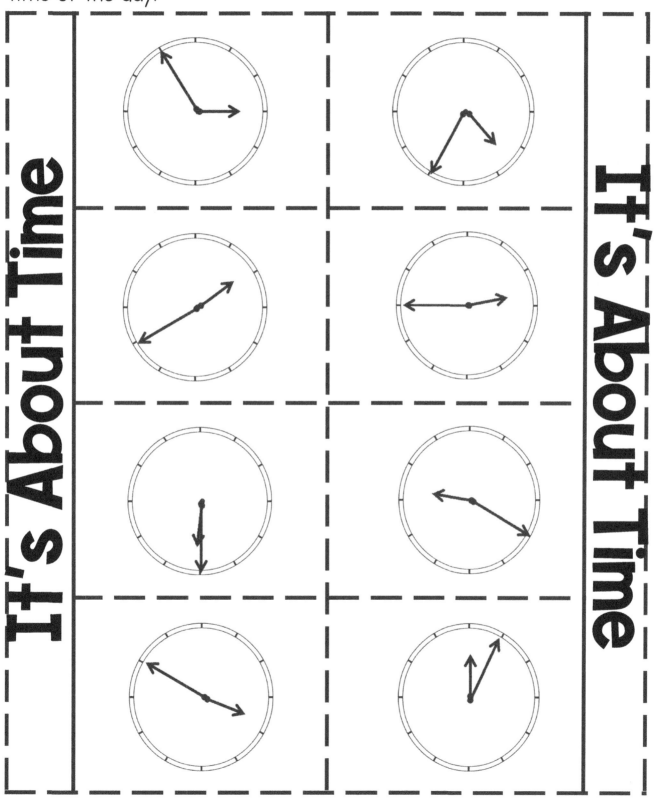

Measure & Plot

Directions: Cut out the graph below and glue it into your notebook. Take a survey of the measurement of pencils of each student in your classroom. Use that data to complete the line plot with an X for each student.

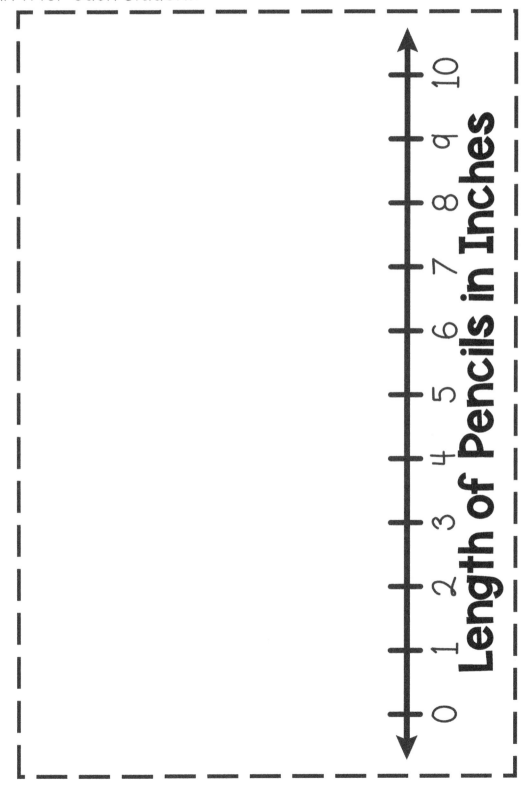

Favorite Subject

Directions: Cut out the graph and journal and glue them into your notebook. Survey your classmates to see how their favorite subject. Draw a picture for each student who likes that subject. Answer the journal question based on your data.

What's Your Favorite Subject?

Math	Reading	Science

Our class has _____ who like math, _____ who like reading, and _____ who like science. The difference between the largest and smallest is _____.

Constructing Shapes

Directions: Cut out the foldable below on the dashed lines. Glue into your notebook under the title section. Under each flap, illustrate the shape and describe the attributes of the shape.

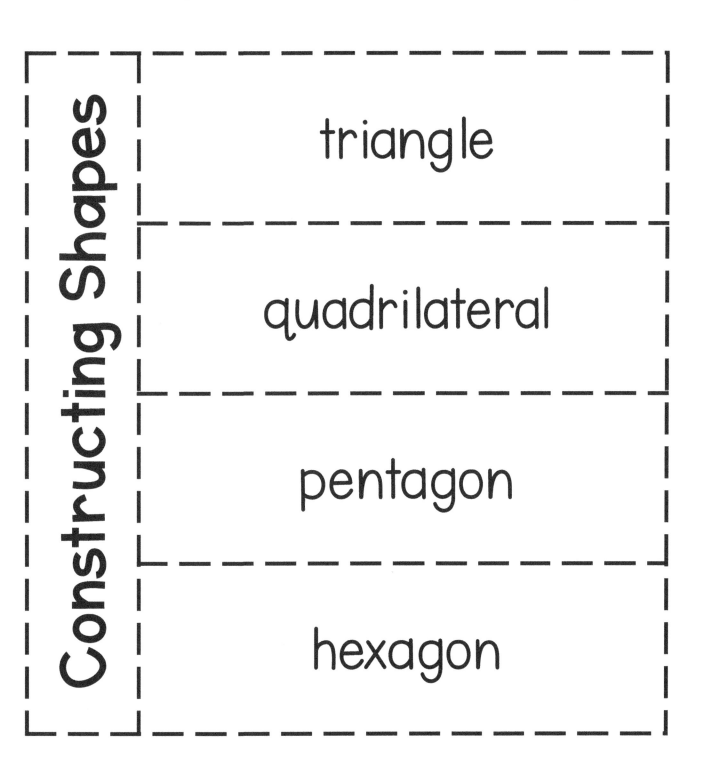

Constructing Shapes

triangle

quadrilateral

pentagon

hexagon

Pieces of a Whole

Directions: Cut out the layered book below and staple it where indicated. For each rectangle divide to form squares of the same size using rows and columns. Record your answer on each page.

STAPLE HERE

STAPLE HERE

Pieces of a Whole

How many same size shape do you have? _____

STAPLE HERE

How many same size shape do you have? _____

STAPLE HERE

How many same size shape do you have? _____

Let's Eat Cake

Directions: Cut out each of the pages of the mini-book below and staple where directed. Draw a line on the cake to show the cake cut in half or fourths. Complete each sentence by counting the parts and coloring each part a different color.

The cake has ___ parts when cut in half.

The cake has ___ parts when cut in fourths.

The cake has ___ parts when cut in half.

The cake has ___ parts when cut in fourths.

Types of Shoes

Directions: Cut out the graph and journal and glue them into your notebook. Survey your classmates to see what type of shoes they are wearing and complete the bar graph. Answer the journal question based on your data.

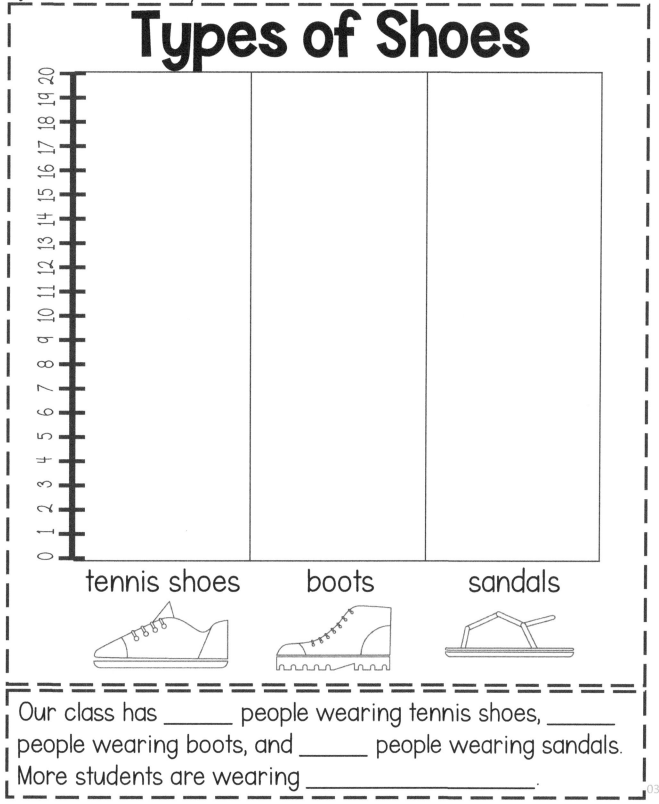

Types of Shoes

Our class has _____ people wearing tennis shoes, _____ people wearing boots, and _____ people wearing sandals. More students are wearing _____.

Creating with Shapes

Directions: Cut out the quilt below. Draw at least 12 different shapes of different sizes to fill in the quilt. Color the shapes. Write an observation about your completed quilt based on the amount of space taken up on your quilt by various shapes.

Odd/Even Sort

Directions: Cut all the cards out as well as the labels. Sort the cards into the given groups based on their common attribute. Use the labels to title your sorts before attaching to your notebook.

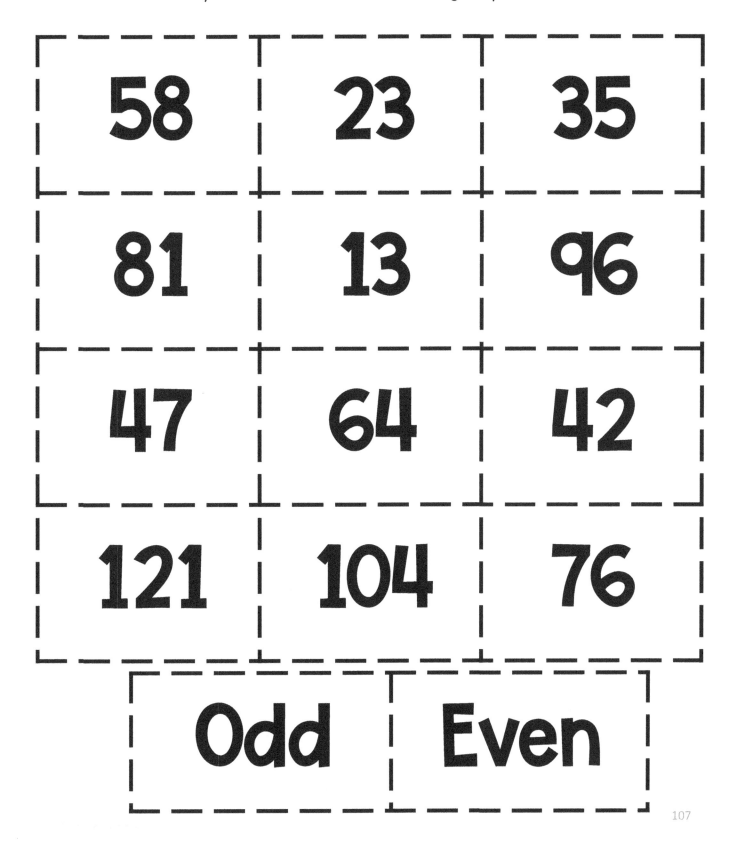

58	23	35
81	13	96
47	64	42
121	104	76

Odd	Even

Odd & Even Roll

Directions: Cut out the tally sheet below. Glue into your notebook. Roll two dice and add. If the sum is even, put a tally mark under even. If the sum is odd, put a tally mark under odd. Repeat for a total of 9 times. Write a sentence about your results.

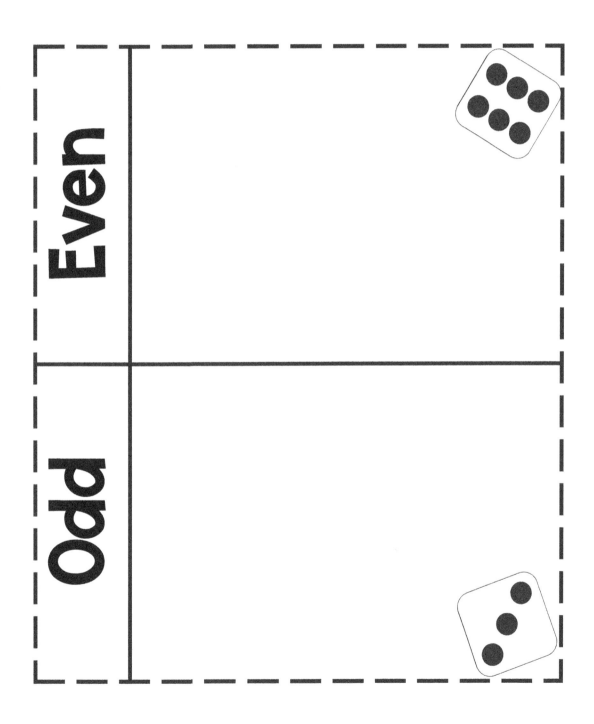

Building Arrays

Directions: Cut out the foldable below. Glue to your notebook under the title tab. Read each flap. Illustrate and write an addition sentence to determine the total under the flap.

Building Arrays

3 groups of 4

4 groups of 2

5 groups of 3

2 groups of 5

1 group of 4

3 groups of 1

Acting Out Multiplication

Directions: Cut out the flip books below. Glue along the tab in your notebook. Read the sentence on the front of each mini-book. Illustrate the sentence below the flap by building an array with stickers.

Cut the foldable on the dashed lines. Fold on the solid lines.

This side should be facing your notebook when glues in and will not be seen.

2 rows with 3 stickers each

Cut the foldable on the dashed lines. Fold on the solid lines.

This side should be facing your notebook when glues in and will not be seen.

3 rows with 5 stickers each

Cut the foldable on the dashed lines. Fold on the solid lines.

This side should be facing your notebook when glues in and will not be seen.

4 rows with 2 stickers each

Cut the foldable on the dashed lines. Fold on the solid lines.

This side should be facing your notebook when glues in and will not be seen.

5 rows with 2 stickers each

Array Match Up

Directions: Cut all the cards out as well as the labels. Find the multiplication sentence that matches the correct pictorial array model. Glue them next to each other in your notebook.

4 x 8	7 x 7		
5 x 3	1 x 12		
2 x 9	3 x 5		
3 x 3	2 x 2		
3 x 4	2 x 5		

What's On Your Pizza?

Directions: Cut out the graph and journal and glue them into your notebook. Survey your classmates to see how their favorite pizza topping. Draw a picture for each student who likes that topping. Answer the journal question based on your data.

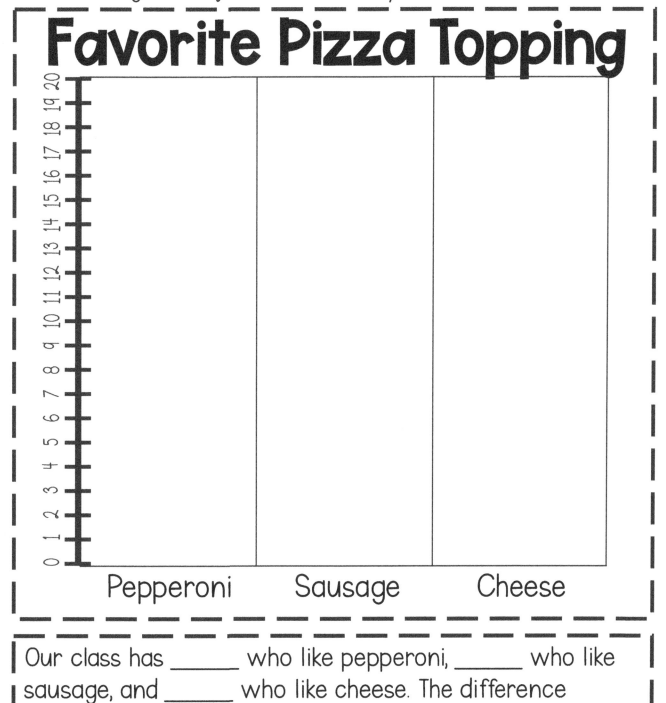

Favorite Pizza Topping

| Pepperoni | Sausage | Cheese |

Our class has _____ who like pepperoni, _____ who like sausage, and _____ who like cheese. The difference between the largest and smallest is _____.

ABOUT ME:

Hey Friends!

My name is Jennifer Jochen (like ocean, with a J) and I am so happy that you chose to download one of my resources to use with your student(s) or child(ren).

I am a certified Elementary, Middle School, Math, ESL and Special Education teacher from the great state of Texas! I started my journey in education in 2003 and have had the privilege of teaching everything from Pre-K (summer school) to College, self-contained to inclusion, one-on-one Functional Life Skills to College Prep. I truly enjoy the diversity and have never met a challenge I wouldn't accept.

As a teacher I quickly learned that no two learners are a like and therefore have always constantly been creating activities to meet the needs of each learner that would not only be engaging, but also relatable so that I could hold their attention while working on a subject like math.

I truly enjoy writing and creating curriculum as much as I do teaching students, and because of this I have also spent time as a consultant working with teachers around the United States to make math meaningful and engaging for their students.

Enjoy my Friend! *Jennifer*

FOLLOW ME:

Facebook: Smith Curriculum and Consulting

Facebook Group: Surviving Sixth, Seventh & Eighth Grade Math

Instagram & TikTok: @JenniferSJochen and @JenniferSJochen

Join the e-mail List: SCC VIPs

YouTube: Smith Curriculum and Consulting

Made in the USA
Las Vegas, NV
22 January 2024

84749948R00066